T0209837

The Me I See
Is The Me I'll Be

Understanding Our Identity

Ronnie D. Henderson, Sr

WestBow
PRESS°
A DIVISION OF THOMAS NELSON
& ZONDERVAN

Scripture taken from the King James Version of the Bible.

Scripture taken from the New King James Version®. Copyright ©
1982 by Thomas Nelson. Used by permission. All rights reserved.

WestBow Press books may be ordered through
booksellers or by contacting:

WestBow Press
A Division of Thomas Nelson & Zondervan
1663 Liberty Drive
Bloomington, IN 47403
www.westbowpress.com
1 (866) 928-1240

ISBN: 978-1-9736-2665-7 (sc)
ISBN: 978-1-9736-2666-4 (e)

Print information available on the last page.

WestBow Press rev. date: 5/1/2018

Contents

Acknowledgements

I would like to thank the LORD for choosing me before the foundation of the world to be in Christ Jesus and inspiring me to write this book.

I would like to thank Pastor Oliver W. Smith for helping me with the editing and encouraging me in ministry over the last seven years.

I would like to thank Minister Linda Warren for also helping with the editing and for the impact she's had on my life.

I would like to thank Loretta Parnell for helping me choose a book cover design and for all the selfless help she has provided for me over the years.

Thanks to the members of Abundant Life Church for helping to get this book published. You are some of the best members a pastor can have. You have made it very easy to lead and it's been a pleasure doing so.

In honor of my parents, Evangelist Eunice Henderson and Walter "Buddy" Henderson, who are deceased, I would like to thank them for the example they set for me and my siblings. I would like to thank them for the unconditional love and selflessness they demonstrated to us and introducing us to Jesus.

I would like to thank Pastor Alice Jeter, who is also deceased. She treated me like her son and was one of the first to encourage me to put this material in book form.

Last, but least, I would like to thank my "good thang," my wife, my closest friend, Lady Francise Henderson. She has stood by me and with me as I navigated through fulltime ministry. She has listened to and encouraged me when I needed it the most. I know it wasn't easy for her, but she stayed the course, and for that I am forever grateful.

Introduction

The material in this book comes from a series of messages I taught at Abundant Life Church, in Brookhaven, MS, as well as in other locations in the past. It comes from different times in my life and ministry where The Lord enlighten and encouraged me through His Word and then allowed me to share it with others. After hearing some of the messages, different ones from different places would encourage me to put the **Id**entity Message in some type of book form. So, after some time of being led by The Lord I did.

I believe this book will help believers from all walks of life and across denominational lines to increase their confidence in the Word of God when it comes to knowing who they are in Christ.

I

The Beginning

I believe it's safe to say that a large percentage of Christians struggle with insecurity, rejection, insignificance and low self-esteem. Some who do, stand before the people of God singing and playing musical instruments every week, while others are teaching and preaching the Word of God. Yes, there are apostles, prophets, evangelist, pastors & teachers who have these struggles, but are afraid to admit it.

Singers, musicians, preachers and teachers are trying to help others get free, when they themselves are still bound. Bound by what others think and say about them. Bound by rejection. *(Allow me to share some insight regarding rejection. Rejection is not always bad. Rejection could be God's protection and redirection for your life).* Some of us desire to be accepted by people and different groups so bad that we'll do things to please them even though we know it breaks God's heart. I believe this book will help Christians from all walks of life experience a better quality of life.

The revelation I want to share with you in this book is so vitally important to your spiritual growth and fulfilling your purpose in life, that the devil doesn't what you to know about it. You should know that you have a hidden **id**entity, but the alarming part is, your **id**entity isn't hidden from the devil. He knows more about who you are than you do. The devil and his demons know the authority you have over them. They realize if you ever get a hold of who you are, what belongs to you, and the rights you have in Christ, they will lose their advantage. They will no longer be able to manipulate you into being something or someone other than who you are. So, they'll fight you tooth and nail to keep you from finding that out and walking in this truth. They can no longer hold your past, and your seemingly inadequacies over your head, nor keep you from walking in everything Christ has accomplished for you. This **id**entity message is a message that every believer need to understand and apply, because fulfilling their purpose with confidence is connected to it.

I want to begin with the help of the Holy Spirit to create an image on the inside of you of who you really are. You are a spirit being, you possess a soul and you live in a physical body. You need to say this out loud. Go ahead. "I am a spirit being, I possess a soul and I live in a physical body." Your body is not you. It houses you and your soul. The spirit and the soul are closely connected and can only be separated by the Word of God.

> **Hebrews 4:12 (KJV)**
> *For the word of God is quick, and powerful, and sharper than any two-edged sword, piercing even to the dividing asunder of **soul** <u>*and*</u> **spirit**, and of the joints and marrow, and is a discerner of the thoughts and intents of the heart.*

The soul has several different functions and the one I want to bring to your attention is your imagination. It's a powerful tool that God has given you to help you be and accomplish everything he intended for you to be and accomplish. Let's begin by using "The Green Icing" illustration.

If you and I were discussing what the imagination is and I wanted to demonstrate the power it has, I would ask you to close your eyes. I would then ask you to picture the first layer of a layer cake. I would ask you if you could see it while your eyes were closed? Then I would ask you to use your imagination and add vanilla icing to the top of the cake. Now add another layer cake on top of the other one. I would ask you if you could see that as well. Then I would ask you to add green icing on those two layers. Can you see it? Now what I just did was paint a picture of a very colorful cake on the canvas of your imagination. How did I do it? I did it with words.

> **Hebrews 11:3 (KJV)**
> *Through faith we understand that **the worlds were framed by the word of God**, so that things which are seen were not made of things which do appear.*

And so that's how we're going to create this image of who you are on the canvas of your imagination......... We're going to do it with words from the Word of God.

II

I Am Who The Scriptures Say That I Am

About 13 years ago, I was reading the Gospel of John Chapter One and came across the passage of scripture where the priest and Levites asked John, 'Who Are You"? This question stood out to me and it was as if the same question was being asked me, Ronnie, who are you? I knew some scriptures but wasn't sure that those scriptures included me. After reading the passages in John Chapter One, that asked who are you, I was inspired to search and understand my own **id**entity.

In the Gospel of John Chapter One, the priests and Levites were sent to investigate John. They knew the scriptures spoke of the Messiah coming and they were curious to see if this might be him. They asked John who he was, and his response was "I am not the Christ". John knew who he was, therefore, he knew who he was not. When you know who you are, you'll know who you're not. This is vitally important for you to know, when it comes to fulfilling your purpose in the earth. The enemy nor anyone else will be able to deceive you or talk you into trying to be someone you're not. John knew who he was. It's likely John's parents told him the story and prophetic word surrounding his birth over and over again and this instilled tremendous confidence in him. It would be wise if believing parents start early doing the same with their children until they understand who they are. If we don't shape their **id**entity, someone else will.

There were two important questions asked of John in these passages. First, who are you? Second, what do you say about yourself? Others will size you up and have plenty to say about you, but what really matters is what you say about yourself. So, who are you and what should you say about yourself? John answered both questions in John 1:23.

> **John 1:23 (KJV)**
> *He said, I am the voice of one crying in the wilderness, Make straight the way of the Lord, as said the prophet Esaias.*

Johns' answer to them was I am who the scriptures say that I am, and I say what the scriptures have already said about me. In v23, John is referring to Isaiah 40:3 that speaks of him and his purpose. John found himself in the Word of God and used the Word to prove who he is. Wow, what a wonderful revelation this is. Just like John, you and I were in the scriptures before we ever showed up in the earth, and we too must use the Word of God as proof of our **id**entity. The Word of God is your **I.D**. It is the proof that you need to say who you are. Again, in v23 John said, "I AM." "I AM" is not past tense nor is it future tense. "I AM" is present tense. John was not waiting to be who the scriptures said he was. He said, right now at this very moment, I am who the scriptures say that I am. It is important to get a hold of this truth that, whoever you are, you are right now. You may not be in your practice, but you are in your position before God.

From Information to Revelation

While further searching the scriptures to find out who I am, I came across **Matthew 16:13-18**. Now, there are plenty of important truths in these passages that I might discuss later, but first I want to show you how to move from information to revelation. You may have heard others mention some of the information you will read in this book, but if you don't have revelation, information is all it will be to you.

Matthew 16:13-18 (KJV)

When Jesus came into the coasts of Caesarea Philippi, he asked his disciples, saying, Whom do men say that I the Son of man am? [14] they said, Some say that thou art John the Baptist: some, Elias; and others, Jeremias, or one of the prophets. [15] He saith unto them, But whom say ye that I am? [16] Simon Peter answered and said, Thou art the Christ, the Son of the living God. [17] Jesus answered and said unto him, Blessed art thou, Simon Barjona: for flesh and blood hath not revealed it unto thee, but my Father which is in heaven. [18] I say also unto thee, That thou art Peter, and upon this rock I will build my church; and the gates of hell shall not prevail against it.

Simon already had the information, the Word, before him, but what he received that day was revelation. This revelation of who Jesus was didn't come from a human but it came from God the Father. [17] Jesus answered and said unto him, Blessed art thou, Simon Barjona: *for flesh and blood hath not revealed it unto thee, but my Father which is in heaven.* You're going to need a revelation from above, to not only know who you are, but to know who Jesus is, and the Father is willing to give you both.

Revelation normally comes after meditation on the information that is before you. You should take the scriptures on who you are in Christ and meditate on them day and night in your mind. You should study to see how they fit with other scriptures that mention "In Christ" and "In Him."

Revelation Word: The word revelation comes from the word reveal which means to uncover; uncover what has been veiled or covered up; to disclose, make bare; to make known, make manifest, disclose what before was unknown. And so, our definition of the word revelation is the word of God uncovered and made known to the believer, by the Spirit of God. It is the illumination of God's Word; understanding of the written word *(logos)* of God given to the believer by God. **Revelation brings resolution**. So, when you receive revelation nobody can talk you out of it, not even the devil.

III

Say Who The Scriptures Say You Are

In chapter two we looked at two questions John was asked by the priest and Levites and they were "who are you" and "what do you say about yourself?" We saw the answer John gave to them both. John said who he was, and who he was, was written in the scriptures. You and I must find out who we are from the scriptures and say who we are. Jesus said who he was, and we should follow in his steps. He said things like, I am the bread of life which came down from heaven. I am the Son of God. I am the way the truth and the life. I am the true vine. I am the good shepherd that gives his life for the sheep. I am the resurrection and the life. I am anointed.

When I mention the word "say," it's another way to describe confess, because that's what we're doing. We're confessing to ourselves and over ourselves. The word "confess" in the Greek means to say the same thing. So, when you believe the Word of God on who you are and say it, you're confessing (saying) the same thing that God says about you. That's what John did. You might say, I don't feel comfortable saying that because I don't see it, or I don't feel it or understand how that's possible. Do you remember us discussing meditation earlier and how it leads to revelation and understanding? Part of the meaning of meditation means to say again and again the word in a low voice, and when we do that, we're confessing the Word of God to ourselves and over ourselves.

The Influence of Words

Some years ago, there were those who spoke negative words to me and over my life. Words are powerful. Proverbs 18:21 says that death and life are in the power of the tongue and they that love it shall eat the fruit thereof. So, we can speak life and live or speak death and die. Now, some of the negative words that were spoken to me and over me came from individuals who had little to no influence on me, so it didn't bother me much when I heard them. But then there were others who I held in high esteem, some well-meaning, while others were not, who spoke certain things that influenced my thinking and my behavior. For instance, words like, you're nothing and you'll never be anything. You're not smart enough to pursue that career. You're better suited for a lesser career. I took that as you're going to have to settle for less than the best that careers have to offer, and it affected what I pursued and how I saw myself.

The words spoken over your life yesterday, has a lot to do with where you are today. And the words that you allow to be spoken over you today, will have an impact on where you will be in the future. Speak Gods Word over your life. It will help shape a better image of yourself and a better future for you and those you love.

IV

Where You Are Will Determine Who You Are

Where are you? Yes you. You who are reading this book right now. Do you know where you are? Did you know that it even mattered when it came to your **id**entity? Ok, relax, I'm not asking for your geographical location but your spiritual location. Where are you? In Adam or In Christ?

> ### *1 Corinthians 15:21-22 (KJV)*
> *since by man came death, by man came also the resurrection of the dead. [22] as **in Adam** all die, even so **in Christ** shall all be made alive.*

According to the scriptures, there are only two places that a man can be; that's in Christ or in Adam. All of mankind came from Adam.

> **Acts 17:24-26 (NKJV)**
> *God, who made the world and everything in it, since He is Lord of heaven and earth, does not dwell in temples made with hands.* ²⁵ *Neither is He worshiped with men's hands, as though He needed anything, since He gives to all life, breath, and all things.* ²⁶ **He has made from one blood every nation of men** *to dwell on all the face of the earth, and has determined their pre-appointed times and the boundaries of their dwellings,*

All of humanity was in the loins of Adam. We all came from Him. He was the first man in the earth. We all inherited what Adam passed down to his sons, and his sons to their sons, and so forth and so on. That which he passed down was the sin nature. So, man was permeated, spirit, soul and body, with sin. But those who are born again have the sin nature in their spirits removed. They become new creatures and are placed in Christ, according to 2 Corinthians 5:17 and 1 Corinthians 12:13.

You should know that where you are will determine who you are and who you are will determine what you can truthfully say about yourself. Those who are in Adam can't truthfully say they are the light and salt of the earth. Those who are in Adam can't say they are the righteousness of God. Those who are still in Adam can't truthfully say they are children of God, because Galatians 3:26 says we become children of God by exercising faith in Christ Jesus. So, where you are will determine who you are and who you are will determine what you can truthfully say or confess about yourself.

So, I'll ask you again, where are you? In Christ or in Adam? If you're still in Adam, according to Ephesians 2:1-2, you're dead in trespasses and sin. You're controlled by the prince of the power of the air. But know that all of this can change if you like. You must choose to move from being dead in Adam to being made alive in Christ. I believe if you're willing to change and you'll sincerely pray this prayer, you will be saved and your position before God will change instantly from being in Adam to being in Christ. Pray this prayer: God, I realize that I'm a sinner and in need of a Savior, and I believe Jesus is that Savior. God, I no longer want to live the way I've been living, I want my life changed and I need your help. I ask you to forgive me for anything and everything I've ever done? I now confess Jesus Christ as my Lord and I believe you raised him from the dead, and now according to you who cannot lie, I am saved. I've been moved from being in Adam to being in Christ. Amen.

And for those of us who are in Christ, let's pray for the opportunity to inform the lost of who they are and where they are. Please understand that it is just as important for the lost to know who they are and where they are headed as it is for Christians to know who they are and where they are headed. **God loves the sinner just as much as He loves the believer.**

As stated in chapter three, you need to locate scriptures with the phrases in Christ and in Him. These scriptures will not only reveal who you are, but they also reveal where you are and what belongs to you.

V

You're Not Who You Use to Be

One day my wife and I got a visit from a lady friend we use to know and hangout with before we were Saved. Before my wife and I married, we lived together. We used foul language, listen to a different type of music, and we were involved in some things that were not pleasing to our families, not to mention God. So, when our friend came to visit us, things had changed. There was no foul language; no secular music; and, no hanging out late at night. All the things our friend thought she knew about us had changed, even our appearance. Before, I was really thin. Some people said that I was so thin, that if I turned sideways, I would disappear. I was "Po" not skinny, but "Po". Po is skinner that skinny. As a matter of fact, my friends called me "Po-Bird". Those who see me now and never knew my given name still call me Bird or Fat Bird. The point I'm trying to make here is that I had changed. The lady friend who came to visit early in the afternoon, even came to our bible study that night. She came back to our home after bible study and talked with the both of us. She saw people who were different. It was obvious to her that **"WE WERE NOT WHO WE USE TO BE."**

Read 1 Samuel 10:1-6

> *1 Samuel 10:1-6 (KJV)*
> *¹ Samuel took a vial of oil, and poured it upon his head, and kissed him, and said, Is it not because the LORD hath anointed thee to be captain over his inheritance? ² When thou art departed from me to day, then thou shalt find two men by Rachel's sepulchre in the border of Benjamin at Zelzah; and they will say unto thee, The asses which thou wentest to seek are found: and, lo, thy father hath left the care of the asses, and sorroweth for you, saying, What shall I do for my son? ³ Then shalt thou go on forward from thence, and thou shalt come to the plain of Tabor, and there shall meet thee three men going up to God to Bethel, one carrying three kids, and another carrying three loaves*

of bread, and another carrying a bottle of wine: [4] And they will salute thee, and give thee two loaves of bread; which thou shalt receive of their hands. [5] After that thou shalt come to the hill of God, where is the garrison of the Philistines: and it shall come to pass, when thou art come thither to the city, that thou shalt meet a company of prophets coming down from the high place with a psaltery, and a tabret, and a pipe, and a harp, before them; and they shall prophesy: [6] And the Spirit of the LORD will come upon thee, and thou shalt prophesy with them, and shalt be turned into another man.

I was somewhat like Saul in 1 Samuel 9:20-21. I didn't believe that God could use me to lead his people and do great things, because of the way I saw myself and because of my past. According to world standards I was uneducated; I only finished high school. As a matter of fact, I spent two years in the 12th grade; not because I couldn't do the work....... I just didn't! As a matter of fact, I make light of this now. I jokingly mention that I have an advantage on those who graduated after only one year in 12th grade. I say, I'm the only one I know who has two senior classes and can attend two class reunions. My past is one of drug and alcohol, pornography, and not being able to keep a steady job. Guilt and shame controlled my thinking. So, after I accepted Christ into my life and was born again, I didn't think God could use me; but, I sure wanted Him to. Then one day I heard God say on the inside of me: "You're not who you use to be, you've been turned into another man." After hearing this, I got my Strong Concordance and looked for similar words in the bible and I found them in 1 Samuel 10.

> **1 Samuel 10:6 (KJV)**
> *And the Spirit of the LORD will come upon thee, and thou shalt prophesy with them, and shalt be **turned into another man**.*

Samuel says to Saul that you will be turned into another man. In other words, you will not be the same person you were. You will be someone you have never been before. You **will not** be who you use to be. WOW! Can you imagine how excited I was to see the very words I heard inside of me and now they are right there in front of me? **Can you imagine how this revelation changed me?**

Those who knew Saul prior to the Spirit coming upon him noticed a change in him.

> **1 Samuel 10:11 (KJV)**
> *And it came to pass, when all <u>that knew him beforetime</u> saw that, behold, he prophesied among the prophets, then*

> *the people said one to another, What is*
> *this that is come unto the son of Kish? Is*
> *Saul also among the prophets?*

The people knew how Saul was and now he was not the same man as before. **Now** the *agent* that God used to turn him into another man was the "Spirit of the Lord". Those who knew me noticed a change in me as well. I stopped doing drugs and didn't drink anymore. I stop cursing and stop going to the night clubs. No more porn and I moved out of the house that I was sharing with my now wife and started attending the church that I now Pastor. Praise The Lord!

The New Creation

> ### 2 Corinthians 5:17 (KJV)
> *Therefore if any man be in Christ, he is*
> *a new creature: old things are passed*
> *away; behold, all things are become new.*

Look at it this way.... If **any** man be **in** Christ, he is a new creation, he is no longer who he use to be, he has been turned into another man. Say this out loud...... Since I am in Christ, I am a new creation, I am not who I use to be, I've been turned into another man. Let's take a closer look at this passage of scripture.

If: the word "if" is followed by a condition that must be met before an individual becomes a new creation, and that is you must be **in Christ.** Your position before God must change from being "in Adam" to being "in Christ".

Any Man: What about an alcoholic, addict, murderer, thief or a robber? What about a person with little or no education? The scripture says…... **any** man. Thank you, Jesus.!!! **WHOEVER WILL………. LET THEM COME.** If **any man** be in Christ, regardless of your ethnicity or skin color, you're **a** new creation, old things have passed away and all things have become new. **New Creation** means a species of being that never existed before.

Mark Hankins said in one of his books, "You are such a different person IN CHRIST, that you will have to let God introduce you to your new self"

One of the first things we can say about ourselves is:

Since I am in Christ, I am a new creation right now. I'm not waiting to be, I already am. You must say this out loud so that you can hear it. Faith comes by hearing the Word of God.

The Part Of Us That's New………Is Spirit

There are some lyrics to an old song that I remember that says, *I looked at my hands and my hands looked new. I looked at my feet and my feet did too.* Well, that's not my testimony. My testimony is that after I was born again, not one part of my skinny little body was new. My hands looked the same. My feet looked the same. I was the same old ruggedly handsome guy I was before my new birth. However, I found out later that the part of me that was new was spirit.

> *John 3:6 says That which is born of the flesh is flesh, and that which is **born of the Spirit is spirit**. {That which is born of the Holy Spirit is the human spirit}*

The way the LORD turned Saul into another man is the same way He will turn you into someone you have never been before…...by the agent of the Holy Spirit.

Man has a threefold nature

> - Man is spirit, he possesses a soul and he lives in a physical body
> 1 Thess 5:23; Heb. 4:12; Roman 12:1,2; Gen. 2:7

Repeat this after me...I am a spirit being, I possess a soul and I live in a physical body.

IMPORTANT NOTE TO REMEMBER!!! Man does not <u>have</u> a spirit …. Man is spirit

VI

You Are A Member

Some years ago, while reading my bible, my attention was drawn to 1 Corinthians 12:12-31. I had read these passages before but now that I knew who I was in Christ, I desired to take a closer look at the passage. When I did this, I saw another aspect of my **id**entity. I realized that I was a member of Christ's body.

> ### *1 Corinthians 12:12-14 (KJV)*
> *For as the body is one, and hath many members, and all the members of that one body, being many, are one body: so also, is Christ. [13] For by one Spirit are we all baptized into one body, whether we be Jews or Gentiles, whether we be bond or free; and have been all made to drink*

> *into one Spirit. [14] For the body is not one*
> *member, but many.*

In verse 12, the apostle Paul, under the inspiration of God, gives an illustration of the human body to the saints at Corinth. He says, the human body, although it has many members, it is just one body, and this analogy is the same with the body of Christ. Christ and the church are one body, a head and many members; made up of many parts yet one body. Verse 13 of this text says, "For by one Spirit are we all baptized into one body, whether *we be* Jews or Gentiles, whether *we be* bond or free; and have been all made to drink into one Spirit."

All the members are baptized into the same body and made to drink of the same Spirit. This word baptized here **must not be** misunderstood and believed to be referring to water baptism. It simply means that once the new birth occurs the Spirit of God placed you into the body of Christ. Some of us were baptized into a local church body before we were baptized or placed into the body of Christ. What I mean is that some denominations will baptize individuals in the water who are not saved. I personally experienced this as a young person when my mother joined a church, and once she joined, I was baptized at this church, but I wasn't saved. I have spoken to others and they have experienced the same or had a similar experience. **People are water baptized and become members of**

local church bodies before they become members of the body of Christ. Local church membership has somehow become more important than becoming a member in the body of Christ.

This is a dangerous practice and could lead some to believe they are saved because they were baptized. I believe this will continue until we begin to see our local churches as a visible representation of the body of Christ. *Ephesians 1:22-23 says, "And hath put all things under his feet, and gave him to be the head over all things to the church, ^{23} Which is his body, the fulness of him that filleth all in all."*

Being baptized or placed into the body of Christ is how we all got in. Jews and Gentiles, slaves and free, educated and uneducated, rich and poor, black and white, Asian and Hispanic. It doesn't matter how you are labeled, if you are in Christ, you got in just like everyone else. You weren't given any special treatment because of your race or your economic status. All of us were baptized into the body of Christ.

In the summer of 2003, a prominent political figure was killed by another political figure inside a government facility. Everyone who entered this facility was required to go through a metal detector. Well, everyone except the politicians. They received special treatment and were allowed to enter in through another entrance which did not have detectors. As a result, one politician was able to bring in a gun and shoot the other. When it comes to special treatment, some of us have been afforded it in society and somehow believe it's going to happen here. But when it comes to getting into the body of Christ, none of us, regardless of our skin color or our money, will receive any special treatment. We all must come through the same door, which is Jesus, and those who do will become members of a new race of people and take on a new **id**entity.

> ***1 Peter 2:9 (KJV)*** – *"But you are a chosen generation, a royal priesthood, an holy* **<u>nation</u>** *(ethnos meaning race) a peculiar people; that ye should show forth the praises of him who hath called you out of darkness into his marvelous light.* **It's time we see ourselves how God see us, and God sees us as** members of a new **<u>race</u>** of people."

You Don't Decide Where You Are Set, You Discover Where You Are Set

As I continued to look closer at what it means to be a member of the body of Christ, I noticed other truths. And one was that since I was a member, I had been set there by God. It seems as if many are just deciding to be a pastor, evangelist, apostle, prophet or teacher. So, they attend schools for a required period and someone dubs them as pastor or one of the others. Know that no amount of education can make someone a pastor. It can surely help, but they must be set in Christ body by God, as a pastor. If not, they will have no grace to pastor. These individuals are simply trying to function from a place that God has not set them. And if you're out of place; you will have no grace for that place.

> ### 1 Corinthians 12:18 (KJV)
> *But now hath God __set__ the members every one of them in the body, as it hath pleased him.*

Therefore, since God had already **set** me, He was the only one who could tell me where I've been **set**. Others may accept and support it, but only God can confirm it. You see, every member has a particular place in the body of Christ, and because of that particular place, they have a particular function. Just like in the natural body, the eyes see for the body. The legs are made to help move the body from one place to the next. The feet are made to support the body as it stands and cooperates with the legs and other parts in transporting the body. Find out where God has set you in the body of Christ and begin to experience God's enabling ability to accomplish his will for your life.

VII

Proper Sight for Leadership

In Numbers 13, after the children of Israel has come out of Egypt, we find them near the border of Kadesh Barnea. And Moses has been instructed to send out 12 spies to spy out the promised land. They were instructed to check out the land, the people, the cities and the forest, then bring back fruit and a report. Let's take up where the spies come back with their report.

> ### Numbers 13:26-33 (KJV)
> [26] And they went and came to Moses, and to Aaron, and to all the congregation of the children of Israel, unto the wilderness of Paran, to Kadesh; and brought back word unto them, and unto all the congregation, and shewed them

the fruit of the land. ²⁷ And they told him, and said, we came unto the land whither thou sentest us, and surely it floweth with milk and honey; and this is the fruit of it. ²⁸ Nevertheless the people be strong that dwell in the land, and the cities are walled, and very great: and moreover we saw the children of Anak there. ²⁹ The Amalekites dwell in the land of the south: and the Hittites, and the Jebusites, and the Amorites, dwell in the mountains: and the Canaanites dwell by the sea, and by the coast of Jordan. ³⁰ And Caleb stilled the people before Moses, and said, Let us go up at once, and possess it; for we are well able to overcome it. ³¹ But the men that went up with him said, we be not able to go up against the people; for they are stronger than we. ³² And they brought up an evil report of the land which they had searched unto the children of Israel, saying, The land, through which we have gone to search it, is a land that eateth up the inhabitants thereof; and all the people that we saw in it are men of a great stature. ³³ And there we saw the giants, the sons of Anak, which come of the giants: and we were in our

> *own sight as grasshoppers, and so we*
> *were in their sight.*

We can see from these passages that most of the spies brought back an evil report, but what these passages don't show is that these 12 spies were leaders. To see this, we need to visit verses 1-3 of Numbers 13.

> ### Numbers 13:1-3 (KJV)
> *¹ And the LORD spake unto Moses, saying, ² Send thou men, that they may search the land of Canaan, which I give unto the children of Israel: of every tribe of their fathers shall ye send a man, every one **a ruler** among them. ³ Moses by the commandment of the LORD sent them from the wilderness of Paran: all those men were **heads** of the children of Israel.*

The NKJV correctly translates the word ruler to leaders, and ten of the 12 leaders brought back an evil report. This is important to note because leaders have influence. What they said influenced the congregation to complain against The LORD, Moses and Aaron. It also prevented them from moving forward into the promised land.

Numbers 13:30-31; 14:1-4 (KJV)

[30] And Caleb stilled the people before Moses, and said, Let us go up at once, and possess it; for we are well able to overcome it. [31] But the men that went up with him said, We be not able to go up against the people; for they are stronger than we.

Numbers 14:1-4 (KJV)

[1] And all the congregation lifted up their voice, and cried; and the people wept that night. [2] And all the children of Israel murmured against Moses and against Aaron: and the whole congregation said unto them, Would God that we had died in the land of Egypt! or would God we had died in this wilderness! [3] And wherefore hath the LORD brought us unto this land, to fall by the sword, that our wives and our children should be a prey? were it not better for us to return into Egypt? [4] And they said one to another, Let us make a captain, and let us return into Egypt.

There were several reasons why these ten spies decided not to go into the promised land and I will share a few with you. First, the way the leaders saw themselves was incorrect. Verse 33 says, *"and we were in our own sight as grasshoppers, and so we were in their sight."* The decisions we make in life are not based solely upon the information and proof we may have. But decisions in life are made in part based upon our self-image…how we see ourselves. We can see that the leaders had the promise of God and they brought back proof that the land was exactly like God said, yet they decided not to go in.

Some believers behave like spiritual anorexics. An anorexic is more that someone who suffers with an eating disorder and extremely low weight. An anorexic also has a distorted view of themselves. While looking into a mirror, they will often believe they appear heavier than they are. Why? Because the way they see themselves is misleading. And it doesn't matter what anyone else says, they will make decisions based on their self-image. Well, some leaders are the same. When they look into the mirror of God's Word, they don't see themselves for who they really are. When leaders see themselves incorrectly, they see others incorrectly. If they see themselves as someone who is superior, they automatically see others as inferior. If they see themselves as better than others, it's fair to conclude they will see others as less than themselves.

The second reason these leaders decided not to go into the promised land is they didn't believe the report of the LORD. God had promised to bring them into a land of abundance, and here they were, but they didn't believe it belonged to them. It's dangerous to have people in leadership who don't believe God. I didn't say, don't believe in God, but don't believe and trust him to do what he said. Sure, there will be giants in our promised land but what are they compared to God.

The third reason these leaders decided not to go into the promised land is similar to reason number one, but different. It is because they had low self-esteem. They thought low of themselves. Verse 33 again says *"and we were in our own sight as grasshoppers."* No one, especially leaders should think low of themselves. There are enough people out there who will do that for them. People with superiority complexes, like Pastor Puff Head and Bishop Put Down, will have no problem looking down on you.

Some leaders don't think low of themselves but do think too high of themselves and the apostle Paul admonishes the church at Rome to not do that.

> ### Romans 12:3 (KJV)
> [3] *I say, through the grace given unto me, to every man that is among you, not to think of himself more highly than he ought to think; but to think soberly, according as God hath dealt to every man the measure of faith.*

He didn't say they shouldn't think high of themselves, but not to think more highly of themselves than they ought to think. There is a level of high thinking that every believer should have, but they are not to go beyond that level. It's a level that allows each of us, including leaders, to esteem others higher than ourselves. If you are at that high level, don't prevent others who are not, from arriving at the same level. Reach down and pull them up by encouraging them in the Word of God. So, leaders, let me encourage you to look into the Word of God, which is like a mirror, and allow the Holy Spirit to open your eyes to see your true reflection.

Sometimes if individuals committed immoral acts or something not to smart, their names were left out of the scripture, and that provided a measure of protection for them from the reader. For example, there was a woman who was caught in adultery and her name is never mentioned. But God named all these leaders in Numbers 13, and readers have seen who they were for thousands of years. Ten are looked upon with disgrace and two are viewed as being courageous.

As we lead others, let us use the ten spies in Numbers 13 as an example of how not to see ourselves and how not to lead God's people. May the Holy Spirit enlighten you to see who you really are, so you can be who you really are. The person you see, is the person you'll be.

VIII

You Are Important And Valuable

Matthew 10:29-31 (KJV)
²⁹Are not two sparrows sold for a farthing? and one of them shall not fall on the ground without your Father. ³⁰ But the very hairs of your head are all numbered. ³¹ Fear ye not therefore, ye are of more value than many sparrows.

In these passages, Jesus reveals his awareness, his perfect knowledge and exquisite care of what was of little value. If he is so attentive to sparrows, how much more to His followers. You're important and valuable to Him. The very hairs of your head are numbered and not one of them falls to the ground without him taking notice.

God Reveals How Important and Valuable You <u>Are</u> In His Word

> ### *John 3:16 (KJV)*
> [16] *For God so loved the world, that he gave his only begotten Son, that whosoever believeth in him should not perish, but have everlasting life.*
>
> ### *Romans 8:32 (KJV)*
> *He that spared not his own Son, but delivered him up for us all, how shall he not with him also freely give us all things?*

He loved you so much that He gave his Son to carry your sins in his body; to be beaten by a band of soldiers until he was unrecognizable; to have his back ripped open with many of lashes; to be crucified and die in your place. You don't do those things for someone unless they're important and valuable to you!

The Twenty Dollar Bill:

Over a decade ago, I heard the story of the twenty-dollar bill and have used it periodically to demonstrate how valuable we are to the Lord. The speaker took out a twenty-dollar bill and asked who would take it if he would give it away. Many in the audience responded by raising their hand. He then took the twenty-dollar bill and crushed it with his hands and asked the audience who would take it if he would give it away? Many raised their hand again. He dropped it on the floor and asked the question again. Still many raised their hand. While it was on the floor, he stepped on it and asked the same question. Once again hands were raised. He picked up the twenty-dollar bill, held it high and said, the reason you continued to raise your hand was because the twenty-dollar bill never lost its value. Wow! What a revelation that was. Well, it's the same way with you. Maybe you've been through some tough times and even crushed by some life situations. Maybe you've been dropped, looked down on and even stepped on by those you love or esteem high. If so, it didn't go unrecognized by God. You're just as important and valuable to Him now as you were before you went through those tough times.

The Gold Rush:

One day while spending time with the Lord, I began to have thoughts about the Gold Rush in the 1800's. During that time, men left their families. Husbands left their wives and even entire families packed up their valuables and headed to California. The Holy

Spirit spoke to me and said, those people did not leave their homes and families because of the gold. He had my attention when I heard this because I always thought that's why they left. He said, they left because of the value that was on the gold. He said people would have packed up everything and left if there was enough value placed on the sand. Therefore, it wasn't the gold they left for, it was the value placed on the gold. The value of gold motivated those people to leave their homes and go after it. Likewise, Jesus Christ left his home in heaven, came to the earth in the form of a man, suffered persecution, beatings from man, and yes, the cruel death of the cross. He willingly and legally came into the earth, then paid the price we owed with his life and set us free from the power and penalty of sin. Did he leave heaven because he loved us? Sure, he did. But He also left because he valued us. You are valuable, and it's been proven and documented in God's Word.

Get in the word of God. Look for passages that have the phrases "in Christ" and in Him" in them. Read others material on this subject. Find out who you are and began enjoying life on a whole new level.

Printed in the United States
By Bookmasters